WE THE PEOPLE

Selma's Bloody Sunday

by Lucia Raatma

Content Adviser: Susan Youngblood Ashmore, Ph.D.,
Associate Professor of History,
Oxford College of Emory University

Reading Adviser: Rosemary G. Palmer, Ph.D.,
Department of Literacy,
College of Education, Boise State University

Compass Point Books ✦ Minneapolis, Minnesota

Compass Point Books
151 Good Counsel Drive
P.O. Box 669
Mankato, MN 56002-0669

 This book was manufactured with paper containing at least 10 percent post-consumer waste.

On the cover: State troopers swinging billy clubs broke up a civil rights march in Selma, Alabama.

Photographs ©: AP Images, cover, 5, 11, 21, 24, 25, 33; Prints Old & Rare, back cover (far left); Library of Congress, back cover, 4, 6, 7, 8, 9, 10, 13, 15, 19, 20, 22, 26, 29, 31, 37; Karen Kasmauski/Corbis, 16; Bettmann/Corbis, 17, 27, 30, 32; AP Images/Vicksburg Evening Post, 36; LBJ Library photo by Yoichi R. Okamoto, 39; Andre Jenny/Alamy, 40; AP Images/Dave Martin, 41.

Editor: Anthony Wacholtz
Page Production: Ashlee Suker
Photo Researcher: Robert McConnell
Cartographer: XNR Productions, Inc.
Library Consultant: Kathleen Baxter

Art Director: LuAnn Ascheman-Adams
Creative Director: Keith Griffin
Editorial Director: Nick Healy
Managing Editor: Catherine Neitge

Library of Congress Cataloging-in-Publication Data
Raatma, Lucia.
  Selma's bloody Sunday / by Lucia Raatma.
     p. cm.—(We the people)
  Includes index.
  ISBN 978-0-7565-3847-7 (library binding)
1. African Americans—Civil rights—Alabama—Selma—History—20th century—Juvenile literature. 2. African Americans—Suffrage—Alabama—Selma—History—20th century—Juvenile literature. 3. Selma-Montgomery Rights March, 1965—Juvenile literature. 4. King, Martin Luther, Jr., 1929–1968—Juvenile literature. 5. Civil rights movements—Alabama—Selma—History—20th century—Juvenile literature. 6. Selma (Ala.)—Race relations—History—20th century—Juvenile literature. I. Title. II. Series.
  F334.S4R33 2009
  323.1196'073076145—dc22   2008005731

Visit Compass Point Books on the Internet at *www.compasspointbooks.com*
or e-mail your request to *custserv@compasspointbooks.com*

R0423095549

TABLE OF CONTENTS

A Day to Remember

It was March 7, 1965, just a regular day to most people in
the United States. But on that day, a peaceful protest march
for the voting rights of African-Americans turned into
a day of violence. A group of people in Selma, Alabama,
planned to walk to Montgomery, the state's capital, which

*African-Americans who wanted to vote in Selma, Alabama, were turned away
by the Dallas County sheriff, Jim Clark.*

was more than 50 miles (80 kilometers) away. They wanted to bring attention to the injustice that they faced. They weren't armed, and they weren't asking for trouble. But trouble came.

Before they had gotten very far, the marchers were attacked by Alabama police officers and driven back into

State troopers assaulted the protesters with billy clubs to break up the civil rights march.

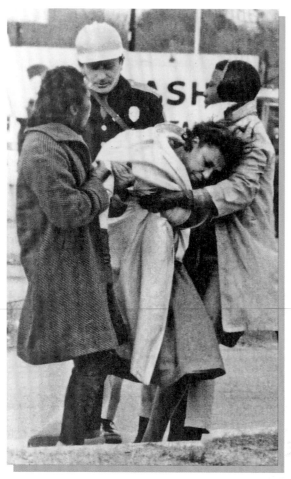

A state trooper watched as two people helped an unconscious victim of the Bloody Sunday attack.

Selma. The protesters were beaten and gassed. They suffered bruises, broken bones, and knocked-out teeth. They gasped for breath and tried to get away from the violent attack by the police. More than 90 marchers were seriously injured, and many were hospitalized. The day came to be called Bloody Sunday.

Across the nation, pictures of the violence were seen by people of all races and backgrounds. Many were outraged by what they saw. They couldn't believe how the marchers had been treated. Suddenly Selma was in the national spotlight, and the civil rights movement had an important stage.

A TIME OF CHANGE

The Civil War was long over, and African-Americans had gained the right to vote. But by the 1950s, there were still many unfair practices, especially in the South. Many cities and states engaged in segregation. Blacks were not allowed to sit in the same waiting areas as whites in bus terminals

A train station in Durham, North Carolina, clearly marked the separate waiting room for African-Americans.

7

African-Americans were required to drink from certain water fountains.

and train stations. They were not allowed to eat in the same restaurants as whites, or at least not in the same sections. Blacks and whites also attended separate schools.

African-Americans often were not treated equally when applying for jobs or trying to rent or buy homes. They had been freed from slavery decades before, but in many ways, they still were not free citizens.

The civil rights movement attempted to change these laws of separation. In 1954, an important Supreme Court ruling—*Brown v. Board of Education*—declared that school segregation was unlawful. The next year, Rosa Parks challenged the rule that blacks were required to sit in the back of city buses in Montgomery, Alabama. Her refusal to give up her seat to a white man led to a bus boycott in that city and gained the civil rights movement national attention.

Rosa Parks (1913–2005) helped ignite the civil rights movement by refusing to give up her bus seat for a white passenger.

Many important leaders encouraged African-Americans to stand up for their rights. A group of people organized the march on Washington in August 1963. The group included A. Philip Randolph, the official director of the march; Bayard Rustin, a co-founder of the Congress of Racial Equality (CORE); James Farmer, president of the Congress of Racial Equality; John Lewis, chairman of the Student Nonviolent Coordinating Committee (SNCC); Martin Luther King Jr. of the Southern Christian Leadership Conference (SCLC); and Roy Wilkins, president of the National Association for the Advancement of Colored People (NAACP). This political rally focused on civil rights and fair housing and jobs.

Roy Wilkins (1901–1981)

At the end of the rally, after a long and exhausting day, King delivered an important speech. Known as the "I Have a Dream" speech, it helped encourage Congress to pass a law ensuring equal rights for everyone. That speech

Thousands of civil rights supporters gathered in front of the Lincoln Memorial to hear Martin Luther King Jr.'s powerful "I Have a Dream" speech.

11

was one reason President Lyndon Johnson signed the Civil Rights Act of 1964. But even after this act became law, King knew that rights were still being denied to many black citizens, so he helped organize peaceful protests.

One very important right is the right to vote. This is a way for people to make their voices heard in the U.S. government. But in 1965, 100 years after the end of the Civil War, many African-Americans were not allowed to register to vote. Local police scared blacks away from voter registration offices. Registrars in the offices tried to prevent blacks from qualifying to vote. They made black people take tests before they could register—tests that other people were not required to take. Many people felt that this injustice could not go on. It was time to bring about change.

THE RIGHT TO VOTE

By today's laws, every U.S. citizen age 18 and older has the right to vote. But this was not always the case. During the time of slavery, black people were not treated as equal citizens of the United States. African-American men gained the right to vote with the 15th Amendment, which was approved in 1870. This amendment to the U.S. Constitution said that no man could be denied the right to vote based on race, color, or having previously been a slave.

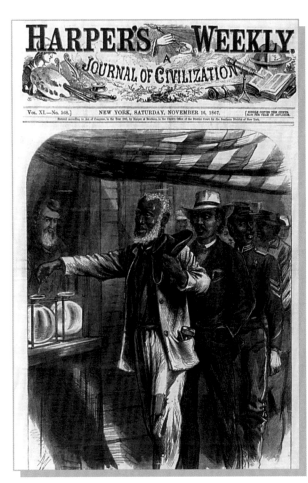

An issue of Harper's Weekly *depicted the first vote cast by an African-American.*

13

In the years after the Civil War, many white people tried to keep black citizens from having the rights to which they were entitled. In some cities, officials did whatever they could to prevent African-Americans from registering to vote. In Alabama, the state constitution of 1901 called for poll taxes that many black citizens could not afford to pay. It also said that some citizens would have to take literacy tests before they could register to vote.

These requirements stopped nearly all African-Americans from voting, even though some of them could read. Registrars sometimes labeled would-be registrants illiterate even if they were not. The fees and literacy requirements prevented a moderate number of poor white citizens from voting, too. This put all the power in the hands of white landowners.

By 1936, many Alabama blacks were struggling to regain their voting rights. In many southern regions, African-Americans attended school for only three or four months a year. The rest of the time, they worked in cotton

Working in cotton fields took time away from education for many African-Americans.

fields or in other jobs. So African-American communities throughout the state established citizenship schools. One leader in this effort was Septima Clark. She helped start these schools and worked to teach people to read. For her efforts, she is sometimes remembered as the grandmother of the civil rights movement.

Septima Clark (seated) and Bernice Robinson were teachers at the first citizenship school.

The citizenship schools helped tutor African-American voters so they could pass the literacy test. The schools also coached potential voters on how to respond to questions asked by voting registration officials. Most important, these schools worked to promote perseverance and pride. Though African-Americans were constantly insulted and turned away at the voting registration offices, they would try over and over again to register. Such persistence was the key to the struggle, and this determined attitude helped begin the 1965 voting rights movement.

In the 1960s, SNCC started a program in Selma, Alabama, to help black citizens register to vote. This group knew that only by voting would African-Americans play a part in the democracy of their country.

At that time, about half of Selma's population was black, but only 1 percent to 2 percent of them had registered to vote. Some residents tried over and over again to register at the county courthouse. The local sheriff, Jim Clark, tried

Sheriff Jim Clark used a nightstick to intimidate African-Americans who arrived at the courthouse to register to vote.

17

to prevent them from doing so, and he instructed all county workers to do the same. The registrars told the black voters that they came on the wrong day, that it was too late, or that the person in charge was not there. So SNCC tried to help African-Americans get organized and stand up against such discrimination.

On February 1, 1965, a large group of blacks gathered at a church and walked to the courthouse to register to vote. However, they were met with resistance. In fact, about 800 people were arrested that day, including Martin Luther King Jr. He noted that "there are more Negroes in jail with me than there are on the voting rolls." When he was released from jail, he went to Washington to insist that President Johnson take action. But no quick action was taken.

More African-Americans tried to register to vote, but few were successful. Most were beaten or arrested by Sheriff Clark and his deputies. Some teenagers who participated in a protest were arrested by Clark and forced to endure a

On February 15, 1965, African-Americans formed a long line outside the courthouse in Selma in an attempt to register.

2-mile (3.2-km) run in the countryside. There is even one story that a 9-year-old boy had to make that run in bare feet.

In nearby Marion, the Reverend C.T. Vivian spoke at a meeting sponsored by the SCLC. That night, as the people left the church where they were meeting, police

C.T. Vivian was leading a prayer outside the Selma courthouse when he was arrested by the sheriff.

officers attacked the crowd. A 27-year-old man named Jimmie Lee Jackson was shot as he tried to protect his mother from being beaten. He died eight days later. It soon became clear that the African-American citizens had to take matters into their own hands. They had to stand up for their rights and insist on being heard.

John Lewis of SNCC and James Bevel of the SCLC worked with King and many others to determine the best

Family and friends gathered at the funeral of Jimmie Lee Jackson on March 3, 1965.

way to protest. After Jackson's death, Bevel remarked that "it would be fitting to take Jimmie Lee's body and march it all the way to the state capitol in Montgomery." That comment led to plans to organize a march. This march would be a way to protest Jackson's murder and demand full voting rights. This would not be just a march to the local courthouse. It would be a march from Selma to Montgomery that would change history.

"AN AMERICAN TRAGEDY"

On March 7, 1965, between 500 and 600 people gathered at Brown's Chapel African Methodist Episcopal Church in Selma, Alabama, and began their march to Montgomery.

George Wallace (1919–1998) was a strong advocate for segregation.

The march was led by John Lewis and the Reverend Hosea Williams, a civil rights leader who was once beaten for drinking from a whites-only water fountain.

The governor of Alabama, George Wallace, said that the march would be stopped, and he sent state troopers to arrest the people who were participating. Wallace enthusiastically supported segregation and fought integration throughout Alabama. He did everything he could to prevent African-Americans from gaining their rights.

As the marchers began to cross the Edmund Pettus Bridge, just six blocks from where they had started, the peaceful protest took a terrible turn. "When we topped the bridge and looked down and saw the sea of blue and the sheriff's deputies and Alabama state troopers on the other side of that bridge, then we immediately knew that there was a problem," remembered Jimmie Wallace, who was one of the marchers.

A large number of state troopers stood shoulder to shoulder across the bridge to block the protesters. Major John Cloud stood in front of the troopers. He ordered the marchers to halt. At that point the Reverend Williams said, "May we have a word with you, Major?" Cloud replied, "There is no word to be had." Then he called to his men, "Troopers advance!"

The marchers faced the troopers for a moment and

tried to continue. But the troopers put on gas masks and moved forward. They began swinging their billy clubs and opened up canisters of tear gas. The protesters moved backward, falling into one another. They stumbled, trying to avoid the beating clubs.

Alabama state troopers wearing gas masks tracked down protesters through a cloud of tear gas.

24

State troopers on horseback oversaw the attack as other troopers swung billy clubs at the demonstrators.

Then from behind the marchers came a group of city police and sheriff's deputies. These lawmen were armed with guns, and some were riding horses. Suddenly they attacked the marchers. The marchers began running back toward the Selma church. But the troopers and other policemen continued to attack them. In addition to the tear gas and billy clubs, they used electric cattle prods and bullwhips. They gassed and beat the protesters, driving them back toward downtown, where the attack continued. Police on horseback pursued the protesters, swinging their whips as they rode. People lay in the street, hurt and bloodied.

In the violence, John Lewis was hit on the head and suffered a fractured skull. Before he was treated for the

Several troopers attacked John Lewis (light-colored coat, center).

injury, he told the crowd, "I don't see how President Johnson can send troops to [the war in] Vietnam … and he can't send troops to Selma, Alabama. Next time we march we may have to keep going when we get to Montgomery. We may have to [go] on to Washington."

The attack was horrible, but news coverage of the event brought about a chance for change. Television cameras captured the violence, and it was shown to the whole world. In fact, television programs were interrupted so news

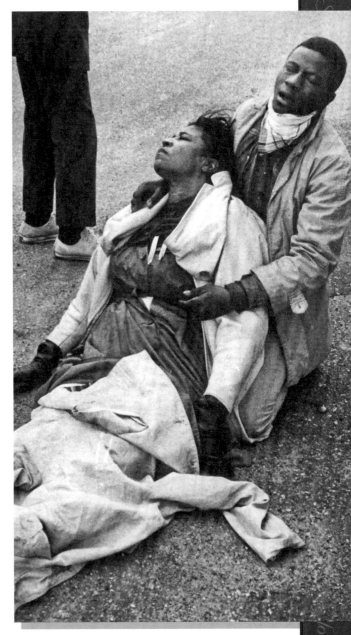

A protester suffering from tear gas exposure held an unconscious woman after the attack.

27

stations could show what had happened. Photographs appeared on the front pages of magazines and newspapers around the world.

Florence Sherman wrote to the editor of *The Washington Post*: "The picture of Alabama State Troopers using clubs, tear gas, and, some say, bull whips on men, women and children was enough to make any decent person feel sick, revolted and furious." People across the United States and elsewhere saw footage of the Alabama police beating the peaceful marchers. Those brutal images inspired support for the civil rights movement. As President Johnson put it, "What happened in Selma was an American tragedy."

SELMA TO MONTGOMERY

Within 48 hours of Bloody Sunday, people in 80 U.S. cities held demonstrations in support of the Selma marchers. King was shocked that the march had turned so violent. He rushed to Selma. King asked people from all over the country to come to Selma and be a part of another protest.

Thousands of people made the trip to Alabama to participate in a second march. The organizers wanted to avoid the violence that occurred before, so they tried to get a judge to prevent the police from interfering. Instead, the judge issued an order to prohibit the march altogether.

A federal marshal read a judge's order to Martin Luther King Jr. (second from left) prohibiting the Selma-to-Montgomery march.

29

This put King and the SCLC leaders in a terrible dilemma. They did not want to defy the judge, but they did not want to give up either. So on Tuesday, March 9, they held a second march. However, the marchers crossed over the Edmund Pettus Bridge and stopped. The leaders held a short prayer service and then turned everyone back to Selma.

State troopers watched as marchers made their way over the Edmund Pettus Bridge.

That day, baseball great Jackie Robinson sent a telegram to President Johnson. His message said: "IMPORTANT YOU TAKE IMMEDIATE ACTION IN ALABAMA ONE MORE DAY OF SAVAGE TREATMENT … COULD LEAD TO OPEN WARFARE BY AROUSED NEGROES AMERICA CANNOT AFFORD THIS IN 1965."

One man who traveled from Boston to participate in the second march was James Reeb. He was a white Unitarian Universalist minister who wanted to work with African-Americans to change the South. The day after that second march, Reeb was attacked and beaten by an

In 1947, Jackie Robinson became the first African-American to play Major League Baseball.

angry white mob. Reeb was taken to Burwell Infirmary, a local hospital. Dr. William Dinkins, a black doctor at the hospital, realized how seriously injured Reeb was and had him transferred to the university hospital in Birmingham. Reeb, who had suffered a massive skull fracture and a blood clot, died on March 11.

The Reverend James Reeb (1927–1965)

People across the country mourned Reeb's death. A week after he died, a federal judge decided that the SCLC was right and that the police could not prevent the group from marching.

On March 21, a third protest march began. This time President Johnson had the Alabama National Guard keep watch and maintain order. Thousands of people

Soldiers from the National Guard lined the route of the Selma-to-Montgomery march.

participated in the demonstration. They were black and white, Jewish, Catholic, and Protestant. After walking for three days, they reached Montgomery on March 24 and camped out at St. Jude, a Catholic center. A rally was held that night, with singers such as Harry Belafonte, Sammy Davis Jr., Tony Bennett, Joan Baez, and Peter, Paul, and Mary performing. The entertainers offered their support

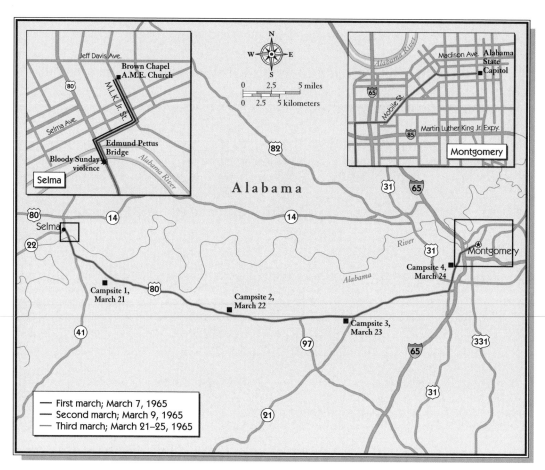

The route the marchers took from Selma to Montgomery was 54 miles (86.4 km) long.

for civil rights and brought more attention to the issue. Their songs of hope and social awareness were heard not only that night but throughout the nation for years to come.

The next morning, King stood near the state Capitol and addressed a crowd that had grown to more than 25,000.

Among those present were Rosa Parks, Roy Wilkins of the NAACP, human rights leader Ralph Bunche, and civil rights leader and union organizer A. Philip Randolph. King said, "They told us we wouldn't get here. And there were those who said that we would get here only over their dead bodies, but all the world together knows that we are here. …" King then went on with his speech: "We are still in for a season of suffering. … How long will it take? I come to say to you this afternoon however difficult the moment, however frustrating the hour, it will not be long, because truth pressed to the earth will rise again. How long? Not long, because no lie can live forever."

AFTER THE MARCHES

While thousands of protesters felt victorious in Montgomery, all was not well. Many white people in Alabama, including members of the Ku Klux Klan, were outraged.

Members of the Ku Klux Klan wore hooded white robes and burned crosses to scare their targets.

They felt threatened by the marches and the idea that blacks should have equal rights. They also disapproved of people from other states coming to meddle in the affairs of their state. The Ku Klux Klan was known for terrorizing African-Americans and anyone who sided with them.

The night after King spoke at the Capitol in Montgomery, a white woman named Viola Liuzzo was driving back to Selma. She was a civil rights activist from Detroit, and a group of Klansmen spotted her Michigan plates. They chased her for 20 miles (32 km) before pulling their car even with hers. They shot her through the window, and she died on the highway. The young African-American man who had been traveling

Viola Liuzzo's car after the attack

with her, Leroy Moton, lay in the car and pretended to be dead when the Klansmen checked on their victim.

The world had watched as the march to Montgomery finally succeeded. But the fight was far from over. There were still people across the country who did not want voting rights to be equal. Some members of Congress were pressured to change the laws to ensure everyone's civil rights. But other members of Congress were pressured to keep things just as they were.

On August 6, 1965, about five months after the marches, President Lyndon B. Johnson signed a historic piece of legislation—the Voting Rights Act of 1965. This law prohibited any unfair practices that would keep citizens from voting. Literacy tests and other discriminatory requirements were made illegal.

In the years after this law was passed, registration of African-American voters increased dramatically. The Voting Rights Act is considered by many to be the single most effective piece of civil rights legislation ever passed

Lyndon B. Johnson shook hands with Martin Luther King Jr. at the Capitol Rotunda in Washington, D.C., where the president signed the Voting Rights Act of 1965.

by Congress. Finally African-Americans had an equal voice in the government.

John Lewis later served as the director of the Voter Education Project. That program helped millions of black citizens register to vote. He also became a U.S. congressman representing Atlanta, Georgia. The 35th anniversary of Bloody Sunday was remembered on March 7, 2000. On that day, Lewis joined Hosea Williams, President Bill Clinton, and others to cross the Edmund Pettus Bridge. When Lewis looked at

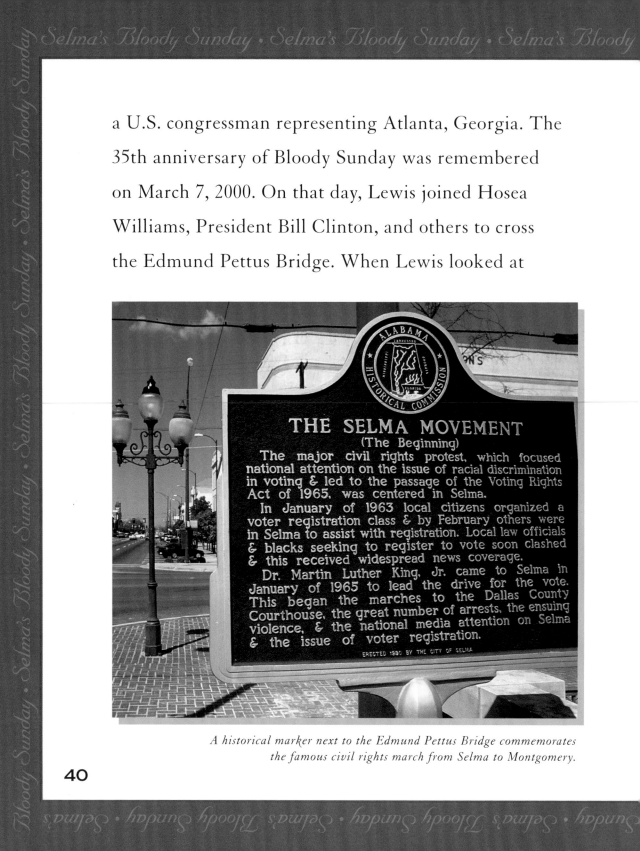

A historical marker next to the Edmund Pettus Bridge commemorates the famous civil rights march from Selma to Montgomery.

Thousands of civil rights supporters crossed the Edmund Pettus Bridge to mark the 35th anniversary of Bloody Sunday.

the crowd that day, he marveled over how things had changed. He observed, "This time when I looked there were women's faces and there were black faces among the troopers. And this time when we faced them, they saluted."

GLOSSARY

activist—person who participates in protests or speaks out in order to bring attention to a problem in society and bring about change

boycott—refusal to use certain services or buy certain goods as a form of protest

civil rights—basic rights that all citizens are entitled to, based on the U.S. Constitution

discrimination—unfair treatment of a person or group, usually based on race, gender, or religion

Ku Klux Klan—group that believes whites are superior to all other races; members terrorize African-Americans and other minority groups

poll taxes—fees that are charged to voters at polling places

segregation—practice of separating people of different races

tear gas—gas that causes people's eyes to be blinded with tears; it is often used to break up crowds

DID YOU KNOW?

- The Edmund Pettus Bridge in Selma was named for a Confederate general in the Civil War.

- In 1964, at the age of 35, Martin Luther King Jr. became the youngest person to receive the Nobel Peace Prize. He won for his efforts to end racial discrimination through nonviolent methods.

- In 1960, there were 53,336 African-American voters in Alabama. In 2008, there were 615,878.

- On November 12, 1996, President Bill Clinton signed a law that designated the 54-mile (86.4-km) historic march route as the Selma to Montgomery National Historic Trail.

- In May 2007, Alabama state trooper James Bonard Fowler was charged with Jimmie Lee Jackson's murder and surrendered to the police.

- A marker in Marion, Alabama, states that Jimmie Lee Jackson "gave his life in the struggle for the right to vote."

IMPORTANT DATES

Timeline

1870	The Fifteenth Amendment to the Constitution grants voting rights to all men.
1901	The Alabama Constitution prevents most African-Americans from voting.
1936	Citizenship schools are established in Alabama.
1954	*Brown v. Board of Education* outlaws segregation in public schools.
1955	Rosa Parks refuses to give up her seat on a Montgomery city bus, which begins a year-long bus boycott; it adds further support to a growing civil rights movement.
1960s	SNCC starts a voter registration program in Selma, Alabama.
1963	Martin Luther King Jr. delivers his "I Have a Dream" speech in Washington, D.C.
1965	On March 7, Bloody Sunday takes place; on March 21, the historic march from Selma to Montgomery begins; on August 6, the Voting Rights Act of 1965 is signed.

IMPORTANT PEOPLE

MARTIN LUTHER KING JR. (1929–1968)

Baptist minister and a leader of the civil rights movement; he was named Man of the Year by Time *magazine in 1963; for his efforts to end segregation, he received the Nobel Peace Prize in 1964; he was assassinated on April 4, 1968*

JOHN LEWIS (1940–)

Civil rights leader and an organizer of the first Selma march; he was chairman of SNCC and has served the state of Georgia as a member of the U.S. House of Representatives since 1987

GEORGE WALLACE (1919–1998)

Governor of Alabama who supported segregation and tried to stop the march to Montgomery; he was elected governor of the state four times and ran for president of the United States; he was paralyzed from the waist down in 1972 after being shot during an assassination attempt

HOSEA WILLIAMS (1926–2000)

Minister and leader of the SCLC and NAACP who led the first Selma march; he founded Hosea Feed the Hungry and Homeless, a nonprofit organization that assists those in need

WANT TO KNOW MORE?

More Books to Read

Bausum, Ann. *Freedom Riders: John Lewis and Jim Zwerg on the Front Lines of the Civil Rights Movement*. Washington, D.C.: National Geographic Children's Books, 2005.

Bolden, Tonya. *M.L.K.: Journey of a King*. New York: Abrams Books for Young Readers, 2007.

Freedman, Russell. *Freedom Walkers: The Story of the Montgomery Bus Boycott*. New York: Holiday House, 2006.

McWhorter, Diane. *A Dream of Freedom: The Civil Rights Movement from 1954 to 1968*. New York: Scholastic, 2004.

On the Web

For more information on this topic, use FactHound.

1. Go to *www.facthound.com*

2. Type in this book ID: 0756538475

3. Click on the *Fetch It* button.

FactHound will find the best Web sites for you.

On the Road

National Voting Rights Museum

1012 Water Ave.

Selma, AL 36702

334/418-0800

Museum located at the base of
the Edmund Pettus Bridge that
commemorates the historic march

**Selma to Montgomery National
Historic Trail**

7002 U.S. Highway 80

Hayneville, AL 36040-4612

334/877-1884

A 54-mile (86.4-km) trail showing
the route the marchers took

Look for more We the People books about this era:

The 19th Amendment

The Berlin Airlift

The Civil Rights Act of 1964

The Draft Lottery

The Dust Bowl

Ellis Island

The Fall of Saigon

GI Joe in World War II

The Great Depression

The Holocaust Museum

The Kent State Shootings

The Korean War

The My Lai Massacre

Navajo Code Talkers

The Negro Leagues

Pearl Harbor

The Persian Gulf War

*The San Francisco Earthquake
 of 1906*

September 11

The Sinking of the USS Indianapolis

The Statue of Liberty

The Tet Offensive

The Titanic

The Tuskegee Airmen

Vietnam Veterans Memorial

Vietnam War POWs

A complete list of We the People titles is available on our Web site:
www.compasspointbooks.com

47

INDEX

About the Author

Lucia Raatma is a freelance writer who has written books about history, safety, wildlife, and famous people. When she is not researching or writing, she enjoys going to movies, practicing yoga, and spending time with her husband and their two children. She lives in New York.